SARAH MARROW

WARWICK TRAVEL GUIDE

Discover All the Top Attractions, Restaurants, Hikes and Activities to Explore in Warwick and the Surrounding Areas

First edition

This book was professionally typeset on Reedsy.
Find out more at reedsy.com

Contents

1

Introduction

Day Trips: Warwick is the perfect base for exploring nearby attractions. We'll highlight the best day trips just a short drive away.

Best Family Activities: Travelling with kids? We've covered you with various activities that the whole family will enjoy.

Conclusion: Finally, we'll wrap things up with some parting tips and a few insider secrets to help you maximise your stay.

How This Book Will Benefit You

When you finish this guide, you'll feel like a local, ready to explore Warwick with confidence and excitement. You'll know where to eat, what to see, and how to experience the true essence of this charming area. Whether you're an adventurer at heart, a culture enthusiast, or a family looking for fun, this book is designed to empower you to seize every moment.

2

Pre-Trip Planning and What to Expect

Booking Your Flights

Planning your flight to Warwick is the first step in ensuring a smooth and enjoyable trip. Here are some key considerations to make your journey as cost-effective and stress-free as possible.

Peak vs. Off-Peak Travel: One of the most important factors to consider when booking your flights is whether you're travelling during peak or off-peak seasons. Peak times, such as summer, school, and major public holidays, typically mean higher airfare prices and busier airports. If your schedule allows, consider travelling during off-peak periods. This helps you save money and also ensures a more relaxed travel experience with fewer crowds.

Alerts and Aggregators: Flight alert services and fare aggregators can significantly help find the best deals. Websites like Skyscanner, Google Flights, and Kayak allow you to set up alerts for price drops on your preferred routes. These tools compare prices across multiple airlines and travel agencies, giving you a comprehensive view of the available options.

Tuesday Tips: A lesser-known tip for booking flights is to purchase on a Tuesday. Studies have shown that airlines often announce deals on Monday evenings, which leads to increased competition and lower prices by Tuesday afternoon. While this isn't a guarantee, it's a valuable strategy that can sometimes result in better deals.

Flexibility with Dates: Flexibility with your travel dates can also lead to significant savings. You might find cheaper options if you can shift your departure or return by a few days. Many flight booking platforms offer tools to compare prices across various dates. Opting for mid-week flights instead of weekend travel can also reduce costs.

Booking in Advance: Generally, the earlier you book, the better. While last-minute deals do exist, they are rare and can be unpredictable. Booking your flights several months in advance can help lock in lower prices and give you peace of mind as you plan the rest of your trip.

Nearest Airports: When flying into Warwick, you have three main airport options: Birmingham Airport (BHX), East Midlands Airport (EMA), and London Heathrow Airport (LHR). Birmingham Airport is the closest, located about 25 miles away, and offers a good balance of convenience and flight availability. East Midlands and Heathrow are further afield but might provide more flight options or better deals depending on your point of departure.

Baggage Considerations: Be sure to check the baggage policies of your chosen airline. Budget airlines, in particular, often have strict and costly baggage rules. Understanding the weight limits and fees for checked and carry-on luggage in advance can help avoid unexpected charges at the airport. Additionally, packing efficiently can allow you to travel with just a carry-on, saving time and money.

By keeping these tips in mind, you can make the flight booking process smoother and more economical, setting a positive tone for the rest of your trip planning.

Arriving from Outside the UK

Travelling to Warwick from outside the UK involves several essential steps to ensure a smooth arrival and transition. Here's a detailed guide to help you navigate visa requirements, currency exchange, time differences, airport transfers, and car hire.

Visa Requirements: Before you travel, check the visa requirements for your country of origin. Citizens of many countries can enter the UK as tourists for up to six months without a visa, but it's crucial to verify this based on your nationality. Visit the official UK government website or consult your British consulate for the most accurate and updated information. If you need a visa, apply well in advance, as processing times can vary.

Currency: The currency in the UK is the British Pound Sterling (GBP). You should exchange money before you arrive for immediate expenses, such as transportation and meals. ATMs are widely available at airports and throughout Warwick, but be aware of any foreign transaction fees your bank may charge. Some credit and debit cards offer free foreign transactions, saving you money on currency conversion fees, so check with your bank before you leave. Currency exchange services are also available at major airports and in Warwick, though airport rates can be less favourable.

Time Differences: The UK operates on Greenwich Mean Time

(GMT) or British Summer Time (BST) during daylight saving months. Check the current time difference between the UK and your home country to adjust your plans accordingly. Jet lag can be challenging, so consider allowing yourself a day to acclimate if you arrive from a significantly different time zone.

Travelling from the Airport: Upon arrival, you must decide how to travel to Warwick. Here are the main options:

Train: From Birmingham Airport, you can take a direct train to Warwick, which typically takes 1 hour. From London Heathrow, you'll need to travel into central London and then take a train to Warwick, which can take approximately 2-3 hours, depending on connections.

Bus: National Express and other coach services run from major airports to Warwick. This option is often more economical, though it may take longer than the train.

Taxi or Rideshare: Taxis are available at all airports but can be expensive. Rideshare services like Uber are also an option, offering a convenient but sometimes costly alternative.

Car Hire: Renting a car is popular, especially if you plan to explore the surrounding areas. Most major airports have a range of car rental companies to choose from. Booking in advance can save you money and ensure availability.

If you decide to hire a car, ensure a valid driving license and an International Driving Permit (if required). Familiarise yourself with UK driving laws, including driving on the road's left side. Car hire companies typically offer GPS rental, which can be very helpful if you're unfamiliar with the area. Ensure you understand the terms of your rental agreement, including insurance coverage and fuel policies.

Addressing these key points can help ensure a smooth transition upon arrival in the UK and a smooth journey to Warwick.

Budgeting for Your Trip

Planning a budget for your trip to Warwick is essential to ensure you make the most of your visit without overspending. Here's a breakdown of the main costs, from flights and accommodation to food and day trips. At the end of the chapter, we'll also provide a rough estimate of the total cost for a 7-day trip.

Flight Costs: Flight costs can vary widely depending on the time of year, how far in advance you book, and your departure location. On average, a round-trip flight to the UK might range from £400 to £1,000. Get the best deals by using fare comparison sites like Skyscanner or Kayak.

● Book at least three months in advance.

● Consider flying mid-week rather than weekends

Cost of Accommodation: Warwick offers a range of accommodation options to suit different budgets. Here's a general idea of what you can expect:

● **Budget Hotels and Hostels:** Prices typically range from £30 to £60 per night.

● **Mid-Range Hotels:** These can cost between £70 and £120 per night.

● **Luxury Hotels and Boutique Stays:** Expect to pay upwards of £150 per night for high-end options.

Booking in advance can often secure better rates, and using sites like Booking.com or Airbnb can help find competitive prices. Additionally, consider staying slightly outside Warwick in nearby towns or villages, where accommodations may be cheaper.

Cost of Food: Warwick offers a variety of dining options, from budget-friendly eateries to high-end restaurants. Here's a rough estimate of daily food costs:

● **Budget:** £10-£20 per day for fast food, casual dining, or self-catering.

● **Mid-Range:** £20-£40 per day for a mix of casual and sit-down restaurants.

● **High-End:** £50 and up daily if you plan to dine in upscale restaurants.

Exploring local markets and grocery stores can also be a cost-effective way to enjoy meals, mainly if your accommodation includes kitchen facilities.

Cost of Day Trips: Day trips from Warwick can add a tremendous variety to your itinerary but should be factored into your budget. Here are some typical costs:

● **Entrance Fees:** Visiting local attractions like Warwick Castle, nearby historical sites, or museums can cost between £10 and £25 per person.

● **Transportation:** Depending on your mode of travel (train, bus, or car hire), day trips can range from £10 to £50 per person. Public transport is generally cheaper, but renting a car offers more flexibility.

● **Guided Tours:** If you prefer organised tours, expect to pay £30 to £100 per person, depending on the destination and inclusions.

Miscellaneous Costs:

● **Souvenirs and Shopping:** Budgeting an extra £20-£50 for souvenirs and local crafts can be a good idea.

● Emergency Funds: Always have a small reserve for unexpected expenses, such as medical needs or last-minute plan changes.

Estimated Total Cost for a 7-Day Trip: Here's a rough estimate of the total cost for a 7-day trip to Warwick, considering mid-range options:

● **Flights:** £400 to £1,000 (average £700)

● **Accommodation:** £70 per night x 7 nights = £490

● **Food:** £30 per day x 7 days = £210

● **Day Trips and Activities:** £40 per day x 5 days = £200

● **Miscellaneous Costs:** £50

Total Estimated Cost: £1,650 per person

Remember, these are average values and can vary depending on individual choices. Adjustments can be made according to personal preferences, but this gives a baseline for what you might expect to spend on a memorable trip to Warwick.

Weather

Understanding the weather in Warwick throughout the year is crucial for planning your trip and packing appropriately. Here's an overview of what you can expect in each season and average temperatures to help you prepare.

Spring (March to May): Spring in Warwick is a beautiful time to visit, with blooming flowers and mild weather. Average temperatures range from 8°C (46°F) in March to 15°C (59°F) in May. Rainfall is moderate, so it's a good idea to pack a light, waterproof jacket or an umbrella. Layers are recommended, as mornings and evenings can be excellent.

Summer (June to August): Summer is the peak tourist season in Warwick, thanks to its warm and pleasant weather. Average temperatures range from 18°C (64°F) in June to 22°C (72°F) in August. July and August are the warmest months, with occasional days exceeding 25°C (77°F). Lightweight clothing, sunglasses, and sunscreen are essential. However, bringing a light jacket for cooler evenings and occasional showers is still wise.

Autumn (September to November): Warwick brings cooler temperatures and beautiful foliage. Average temperatures range from 18°C (64°F) in September to 10°C (50°F) in November. This season can be variable, with warm days early in September and much cooler weather by November. Mixing warm and cool weather clothing, including sweaters and a medium-weight jacket, will help you stay comfortable.

Don't forget a raincoat or umbrella, as autumn can be wet.

Winter (December to February): Winter in Warwick is cold, with temperatures often dipping below freezing. Average temperatures range from 5°C (41°F) in December to 2°C (36°F) in February. Snow is possible, but not every day. Pack warm clothing, including a heavy coat, hats, gloves, and scarves. Layers are essential to stay warm when exploring outdoor attractions.

General Tips: Warwick's weather can be unpredictable regardless of the season, so it's always good to be prepared for rain. Comfortable walking shoes are essential year-round, given the town's charming but sometimes uneven cobblestone streets. Check the weather forecast closer to your departure date to make necessary adjustments to your packing list.

Understanding Warwick's weather patterns will help you pack appropriately and ensure you're ready for all types of weather, making your trip more enjoyable.

What to Pack

Packing for a trip to Warwick requires careful consideration of the time of year and typical UK weather conditions. Here's a guide to help you pack efficiently for any situation.

General Packing Tips: Regardless of the season, there are a few essentials you should always bring:

● **Travel Documents:** Passport, visa (if required), travel insurance, and copies of essential documents.

● **Electronics:** Phone, charger, power bank, camera, and a UK power adapter (UK plugs are Type G with 230V voltage).

● **Money and Cards:** Credit/debit cards, cash in GBP, and a wallet.

● **Daypack:** A small backpack for day trips and excursions.

● **Comfortable Shoes:** Good-quality shoes are essential for exploring Warwick's cobblestone streets and hiking trails. Ensure your footwear is broken in before your trip to avoid blisters.

Spring (March to May): Spring in Warwick is mild but unpredictable, with occasional rain showers.

● **Clothing:** Lightweight layers, long-sleeve shirts, sweaters, and a medium-weight jacket.

● **Footwear:** Comfortable walking shoes and waterproof boots.

● **Accessories:** Umbrella, raincoat, sunglasses, and a hat for sunnier days.

Summer (June to August): Summer is warm and generally pleasant, but occasional rain is still possible.

● **Clothing:** Wear light, breathable clothing such as T-shirts, shorts, and dresses. Bring a light jacket or sweater for cooler evenings.

● **Footwear:** Comfortable sandals and walking shoes.

● **Accessories:** Sunglasses, sunscreen, hat, a small travel umbrella, and a reusable water bottle.

Autumn (September to November): Autumn brings cooler temperatures and can be variable.

● **Clothing:** Layers including long-sleeve shirts, sweaters, and a warm jacket. Pack a few t-shirts for warmer days early in the season.

● **Footwear:** Sturdy walking shoes and waterproof boots.

● **Accessories:** Raincoat, umbrella, scarf, and gloves for cooler mornings and evenings.

Winter (December to February): Winter in Warwick is cold, with temperatures often dipping below freezing.

● **Clothing:** Wear warm layers such as thermal shirts, sweaters, and a heavy coat. Also, wear hats, gloves, and scarves.

● **Footwear:** Insulated, waterproof boots and warm socks.

● **Accessories:** Umbrella, lip balm to protect against cold, dry air, and a thermos for hot drinks.

Additional Tips

- **Layering is essential** for adjusting to the UK's variable weather. It allows you to adapt your clothing based on changes in temperature and conditions.
- **Waterproof Gear:** Always have a waterproof jacket or coat and a small travel umbrella. The UK is known for its sudden rain showers.
- **Reusable Items:** Consider packing a reusable water bottle and shopping bags to reduce waste and stay hydrated on the go.
- **Medications and Toiletries:** Bring any prescription medications you need, along with basic toiletries like toothpaste, shampoo, and a first-aid kit.

By packing thoughtfully and considering the time of year, you'll be well-prepared to enjoy everything Warwick offers, rain or shine. Always check the weather before travelling.

Where to Stay

Warwick offers diverse accommodation options to suit various budgets and preferences. Whether you're looking for a budget-friendly stay, a charming bed and breakfast, or a luxurious hotel, Warwick has something to offer every traveller.

Budget Accommodation: For travellers looking to save money, there are several budget-friendly options available:

- **Hostels:** Hostels are a great option for budget-conscious travellers, offering dormitory-style rooms and shared facilities. The YHA Stratford-Upon-Avon Hostel located a short drive from Warwick, provides affordable accommodation with a friendly atmosphere and basic amenities.

- **Budget Hotels:** Chains like Premier Inn and Travelodge offer reasonably priced clean, comfortable rooms. These hotels are often conveniently located near major attractions and transport links.

Mid-Range Hotels: If you're looking for a balance between cost and comfort, Warwick has plenty of mid-range hotels that provide excellent value:

- **Boutique Hotels:** Boutique hotels like The Globe offer unique, stylish accommodations with personalized service. Located in the heart of Warwick, The Globe features elegantly decorated rooms and an on-site restaurant.
- **Traditional Inns:** Staying at a traditional inn, such as The Rose and Crown, provides a cosy, authentic experience. These inns often have charming historical features and offer hearty meals in their pub-style restaurants.

Bed and Breakfasts: Consider staying at one of Warwick's many bed and breakfasts for a more personal touch. B&Bs offer a homely atmosphere, often with the added benefit of a delicious homemade breakfast:

- **Park Cottage:** This charming B&B is set in a 15th-century timber-framed house and offers a cosy, historic atmosphere with modern comforts. Guests can enjoy a full English breakfast each morning.
- **Cambridge Villa:** Located just a short walk from Warwick town centre, Cambridge Villa offers comfortable rooms and a welcoming environment. The hosts provide excellent local knowledge and a hearty breakfast to start your day.

High-End Hotels: For those seeking luxury and top-notch amenities, Warwick has several high-end hotels that cater to a more upscale experience:

- **The Warwickshire Hotel & Country Club:** This luxurious hotel features spacious rooms, an on-site golf course, a spa, and fine dining options. It's perfect for travellers looking to relax and enjoy various amenities.
- **Mallory Court Country House Hotel & Spa:** Located just outside Warwick, this elegant country house hotel offers luxurious accommodations, beautiful gardens, and a world-class spa. The hotel's fine dining restaurant serves exquisite cuisine from locally sourced ingredients.

Alternative Accommodations: For something a little different, consider these alternative lodging options:

- **Self-Catering Cottages:** Renting a self-catering cottage is ideal for families or groups who prefer a home-away-from-home experience. These cottages offer full kitchens and ample living space. Options like The Old Post Office in the nearby village of Wellesbourne provide a charming and comfortable stay.
- **Camping and Glamping:** For outdoor enthusiasts, Warwick and its surrounding areas offer several campsites and glamping options. Riverside Park in Stratford-upon-Avon offers riverside pitches and luxury glamping pods for a unique, nature-filled experience.

By considering the range of accommodation options available, you can choose the perfect place to stay that fits your budget and preferences.

How Long Should I Stay?

The length of your stay in Warwick depends on how much you want to explore. Here's a guide to help you decide.

Day 1:

- Explore Warwick Castle.
- Stroll through the town centre.
- Visit St. Mary's Church and the Lord Leycester Hospital.
- Dine at a local pub.

Day 2: Take a day trip to Stratford-upon-Avon to visit Shakespeare's Birthplace, Anne Hathaway's Cottage, and the Royal Shakespeare Theatre.

Day 3: Hike in the Cotswolds, visit Hidcote Manor, or stroll along the River Avon. Return to Warwick for dinner and a ghost tour.

Day 4: Visit Kenilworth Castle and Leamington Spa, known for their parks, Regency architecture, and the Royal Pump Rooms.

Day 5: Spend the day at Charlecote Park, exploring the historic house, beautiful gardens, and deer park.

Day 6: Explore the wider region, such as Bicester Village for shopping or Oxford for its historic university and architecture.

Day 7:

- Relax in Warwick.
- Revisit favourite spots or discover new ones.
- Enjoy the local markets or parks.

Conclusion

The ideal length of stay in Warwick depends on your interests and desired depth of exploration. A short visit offers a great introduction,

Managing Jet Lag: Jet lag can be a common challenge when travelling across time zones. Here are some practical tips to help you manage and minimize the effects of jet lag so you can fully enjoy your time in Warwick.

Adjust Your Schedule Before You Leave:

- **Gradual Adjustment:** A few days before your trip, adjust your sleep schedule to match Warwick's time zone. Go to bed and wake up an hour earlier or later each day to ease the transition.
- **Meal Times:** Similarly, adjust your meal times to align more closely with those in Warwick. This helps your body clock adapt more

smoothly.

During the Flight:

- **Stay Hydrated:** Drink plenty of water during your flight to stay hydrated. Avoid alcohol and caffeine, as they can dehydrate you and disrupt your sleep patterns.
- **Sleep Strategically:** If it's nighttime in Warwick, try to sleep during the flight. Use an eye mask, earplugs, and a neck pillow to create a comfortable sleep environment.
- **Move Around:** Periodically stand up, stretch, and walk around the cabin to improve circulation and reduce fatigue.

Upon Arrival:

- **Get Some Sun:** Exposure to natural light helps reset your internal clock. Spend time outside, especially in the morning, to help adjust to the new time zone.
- **Stay Awake Until Local Bedtime:** Resist the urge to nap upon arrival. Staying awake until the local bedtime will help you adjust quickly to the new schedule.
- **Keep Active:** Engage in light physical activities such as walking or exploring the town. Exercise can boost your energy levels and help regulate your sleep-wake cycle.

Maintain a Healthy Routine:

- **Balanced Diet:** Eat nutritious meals regularly to help your body adjust. Avoid heavy meals close to bedtime.
- **Stay Hydrated:** Continue drinking plenty of water throughout your stay to stay hydrated and alert.

- **Relax Before Bed:** Create a calming pre-sleep routine. Avoid screens and consider reading a book or taking a warm bath to wind down.

Consider Natural Sleep Aids:

- **Melatonin:** Melatonin supplements can help regulate your sleep cycle. Take them as a healthcare professional advises, ideally an hour before bedtime in Warwick.
- **Herbal Remedies:** Herbal teas such as chamomile or valerian root can promote relaxation and help you fall asleep more easily.

By following these tips, you can minimize the effects of jet lag and quickly adapt to Warwick's time zone, ensuring you're well-rested and ready to explore

Transport to Your Hotel/Airbnb

Once you arrive in Warwick, your first task is to get from your point of arrival to your accommodation. Here are some local transport options to help you make this journey as smooth as possible.

Local Transportation in Warwick: Warwick offers several convenient ways to reach your hotel or Airbnb:

- **Walking:** If your accommodation is close to the town centre or train station, walking might be the most accessible and enjoyable option. Warwick's charming streets are pedestrian-friendly, allowing you to start soaking in the local atmosphere immediately.
- **Buses:** Local buses connect parts of Warwick and nearby areas such as Leamington Spa and Stratford-upon-Avon. Check the latest timetables and routes on the Warwickshire County Council website or at local bus stops.
- **Taxis/Rideshare:** Taxis are readily available at key locations like

the train station and main bus stops. Alternatively, rideshare services such as Uber operate in Warwick and can be booked via their respective apps for convenience and ease of use.

- **Bicycle Rentals:** Consider renting a bicycle for a more active and eco-friendly option. Some local shops offer bike rentals, and cycling can be a great way to explore Warwick and its scenic surroundings at your own pace.

Getting to your accommodation efficiently will help you start your trip on the right foot, allowing you to relax and begin exploring Warwick without delay.

Supermarket/Non-Restaurant Food Options

Exploring supermarket and non-restaurant food options in Warwick is a great way to save money and enjoy a variety of local and international foods. Here's a guide to what's available:

Supermarkets: Warwick has several supermarkets where you can purchase groceries, ready-to-eat meals, and snacks:

- **Tesco Superstore:** Located on Emscote Road, Tesco offers a wide range of products, including fresh produce, bakery items, ready meals, and beverages. You'll also find a selection of international foods and essential household items.
- **Sainsbury's:** Situated in Saltisford, Sainsbury's provides various groceries, organic options, and pre-packaged meals. The store also has a pharmacy and a café.
- **Waitrose:** Found in nearby Kenilworth, Waitrose is known for its high-quality products, including fresh produce, speciality foods, and an extensive wine selection. It's an excellent option for those looking for gourmet items.

Convenience Stores: For quick stops and smaller purchases, Warwick has several convenience stores:

- **Co-op Food:** Located on Coten End, the Co-op offers a range of essentials, including fresh produce, dairy products, sandwiches, and snacks.
- **Spar:** Situated on Stratford Road, Spar is perfect for grabbing on-the-go items like drinks, snacks, and ready-made sandwiches.

Local Markets: Warwick hosts several markets where you can find fresh, local produce and artisanal goods:

- **Warwick Market:** Held every Saturday in the Market Square, this market offers fresh fruits and vegetables, baked goods, cheeses, and meats. It's a great place to experience local flavours and support small businesses.
- **Farmer's Markets:** Occasionally, Warwick hosts farmer's markets where you can buy locally sourced, organic produce, handmade crafts, and speciality foods directly from the producers.

Speciality Food Shops: For unique and high-quality items, visit some of Warwick's speciality food shops:

- **The Little Artisan Market:** Located on Swan Street, this shop offers a variety of artisanal foods, including cheeses, meats, and baked goods.
- **Wootton Organic Wholesale and Farm Shop:** Situated just outside Warwick, this farm shop provides organic produce, free-range meats, and other farm-fresh products.

Takeaway Options: If you prefer to grab something quick and easy, there are plenty of takeaway options in Warwick:

- **Gregg's:** Known for its pastries, sandwiches, and salads, Gregg's is a popular choice for a quick and affordable meal.
- **Subway:** Located on High Street, Subway offers customizable sandwiches and salads for a healthy, convenient option.
- **Local Fish and Chips:** Many local shops offer traditional fish and chips, a classic British meal that's filling and budget-friendly.

Health Food Stores: For those with dietary restrictions or seeking health-focused options:

- **Holland & Barrett:** Located on Market Street, this health food store offers a range of vitamins, supplements, organic foods, and speciality products for various dietary needs.

By exploring these supermarket and non-restaurant food options, you can enjoy various meals and snacks during your stay in Warwick while keeping your budget in check.

Wildlife to Expect

Warwick and its surrounding areas are rich in wildlife, offering nature enthusiasts a chance to encounter various animals in their natural habitats. Here's what you can expect to see:

Birds

- **Red Kites:** These majestic birds of prey, with their distinctive forked tails and reddish-brown bodies, are often seen soaring over the countryside.
- **Kingfishers:** You might spot bright blue and orange birds darting through the water near rivers and streams.

- **Swans and Ducks:** Common along the River Avon, these water-fowl are a charming sight, especially in areas like St. Nicholas Park and Warwick Castle grounds.
- **Robins, Blue Tits, and Sparrows:** These tiny birds are frequently seen in gardens and parks throughout Warwick, adding colour and song to the landscape.

Mammals

- **Deer:** In the surrounding woodlands and fields, especially in places like Charlecote Park, you might spot herds of fallow and roe deer grazing peacefully.
- **Foxes:** These nocturnal animals are sometimes seen in more rural areas and occasionally venture into town at night.
- **Hedgehogs:** These cute, spiky creatures are often found in gardens and hedgerows, particularly in the evenings.

Insects and Butterflies

- **Butterflies:** During the warmer months, you can see various butterflies, such as the Red Admiral, Peacock, and Painted Lady, fluttering around gardens and meadows.
- **Dragonflies and Damselflies:** These vibrant insects can be seen darting about near water bodies like rivers and ponds, especially in summer.

Amphibians and Reptiles

- **Frogs and Toads:** These amphibians are found in damp areas, gardens, and near ponds. They are most active during the spring and summer months.

- **Grass Snakes and Slow Worms:** While not common, these reptiles can occasionally be seen basking in sunny spots in rural areas.

Fish

- **Trout and Perch:** The River Avon is home to various fish species, and if you enjoy fishing or simply observing, you might spot these fish in the clear waters.
- **Minnows and Sticklebacks:** Smaller fish are commonly found in streams and shallow parts of rivers, providing a glimpse into the region's aquatic life.

Wildflowers and Plants

While not wildlife per se, the flora of Warwick is also worth noting:

- **Bluebells:** In the spring, woodlands like those at Ryton Wood and Crackley Woods are carpeted with these beautiful blue flowers.
- **Wild Garlic:** Wild garlic, recognized by its white flowers and strong aroma, is often found in shady, wooded areas.
- **Hawthorn and Elderflower:** These flowering plants are common in hedgerows and add to the countryside's natural beauty.

Parks and Nature Reserves

- **St. Nicholas Park:** This park in Warwick is home to various bird species, squirrels, and beautiful plant life, making it an excellent spot for wildlife watching.
- **Brandon Marsh Nature Reserve:** Located a short drive from Warwick, this reserve offers diverse habitats, including wetlands

and woodlands, supporting a wide range of wildlife.

Exploring Warwick's wildlife provides a beautiful opportunity to connect with nature and appreciate the region's biodiversity. Whether strolling through a park, hiking in the countryside, or simply relaxing by the river, keep an eye out for these fascinating creatures.

4

The Foods of Warwick

W arwick boasts a rich culinary heritage with traditional English dishes that are a must-try for any visitor. Here's a guide to some of the most delicious English foods you should experience and recommendations on where to find the best in town.

What is Fish & Chips?

Fish and chips is a quintessentially British dish of deep-fried fish, usually cod or haddock, served with chunky chips (fries). Mushy peas, tartar sauce, and a wedge of lemon often accompany it.

Where to Get the Best Fish & Chips in Warwick:

- **The Chip Shed:** Located on Market Place, It is renowned for its fresh, sustainably sourced fish and perfectly crispy chips. Their traditional take on this classic dish is popular among locals and visitors. The Chip Shed offers a budget-friendly dining experience. Main courses typically range from £8 to £15, making it an affordable option for enjoying traditional fish and chips.
- **Robbie's Restaurant:** Situated on High Street, Robbie's offers a cosy atmosphere and serves up some of the best fish and chips in town, with generous portions and friendly service. Main courses typically range from £15 to £25, providing quality meals at a reasonable price.
- **St. John's Fish Bar:** A popular takeaway spot on St. John's Street, this fish bar is known for its excellent quality and quick service, making it a great option for enjoying fish and chips on the go. Main courses typically range from £6 to £12, making it an affordable option for enjoying traditional fish and chips.

What is Pub Grub?

Pub grub refers to the hearty, traditional meals served in British pubs. These dishes are typically filling and flavourful, ranging from pies and stews to burgers, bangers, and mash.

Where to Get the Best Pub Grub in Warwick:

- **The Rose & Crown:** Located in the heart of Warwick on Market Place, this pub offers a warm atmosphere and a menu full of classic pub dishes, including steak and ale pie, fish and chips, and sausages with mashed potatoes, budget-friendly with mains around £10-£20.
- **The Old Fourpenny Shop Hotel:** Situated on Crompton Street,

this historic pub provides a cosy setting and a wide selection of traditional pub fare, including their highly recommended beef and ale pie and hearty Sunday roasts. It typically falls into the mid-range budget category. Main courses usually range from £12 to £25, making it an affordable yet high-quality dining experience.

- **The Tilted Wig:** Found on Market Place, The Tilted Wig is a charming pub with a diverse menu featuring pub classics like fish and chips, burgers, and various pies. Their friendly staff and inviting ambience make it a must-visit. The Tilted Wig offers a mid-range dining experience. Main courses typically range from £15 to £30, providing a good balance of quality and affordability.

What is a Sunday Roast?

A Sunday roast is a traditional British meal typically served on Sundays. It consists of roasted meat (beef, lamb, chicken, or pork), roast potatoes, vegetables, Yorkshire pudding, and gravy. It's a beloved comfort food that brings families together for a hearty meal.

Where to Get the Best Sunday Roast in Warwick:

- **The Globe:** Located on Theatre Street, The Globe offers a superb Sunday roast with a choice of meats, delicious roast potatoes, seasonal vegetables, and homemade Yorkshire puddings. The welcoming atmosphere makes it perfect for a relaxing Sunday meal. Expect to spend around £15 to £20 per person for a full Sunday roast experience.
- **The Warwick Arms Hotel:** Situated on High Street, this historic hotel serves an excellent Sunday roast in a traditional setting. Their generous portions and flavourful dishes make it a favourite spot for locals. Sunday roast typically falls within the mid-range budget category. Expect to spend around £12 to £18 per person for a full

Sunday roast experience.

- **The Saxon Mill:** Just outside Warwick, on Coventry Road, The Saxon Mill provides a picturesque riverside location and a fantastic Sunday roast. The rustic charm and beautiful views enhance the dining experience, making it well worth the short trip. The Sunday roast generally falls within the mid-range to slightly higher budget category. Expect to spend around £18 to £25 per person for a full Sunday roast experience.

Exploring Warwick's food is a delightful way to immerse yourself in English culture and enjoy the town's culinary offerings. Whether indulging in crispy fish and chips, savouring hearty pub grub, or enjoying a traditional Sunday roast, Warwick's food scene will surely leave a lasting impression.

5

Best Restaurants in Warwick

Warwick and its surrounding areas have a vibrant culinary scene, offering diverse dining experiences. From fine dining to casual eateries, there's something for every palate and budget. Here's a guide to some of the best restaurants in the region, highlighting their standout dishes and other essential details.

Chale's Restaurant & Warren's Bar

Overview: Cheal's Restaurant & Warren's Bar is a fine dining establishment in the heart of Henley-in-Arden, within a 10-mile radius of Warwick. Known for its modern British cuisine, Cheal's offers an exquisite dining experience focusing on seasonal and locally sourced ingredients.

Best Dishes:

- **Tasting Menu:** A multi-course tasting menu that showcases the chef's creativity and the best of local produce.
- **Beef Wellington:** A signature dish known for perfectly cooked beef encased in flaky pastry.
- **Seafood Platter:** Fresh and beautifully presented, featuring various finest seafood.

Budget: Dining here is expensive, typically from £70 to £100 per person for a complete dining experience.

Additional Information: The dress code ranges from smart casual to formal. Reservations are highly recommended, particularly on weekends and for special occasions.

The Bluebell at Henley-in-Arden

Overview: The Bluebell at Henley-in-Arden is a charming gastropub offering a relaxed yet sophisticated dining experience. Focusing on British and European cuisine, The Bluebell is celebrated for its innovative dishes and welcoming atmosphere.

Best Dishes:

- **Lamb Rump:** Tender and flavourful, served with seasonal vegetables and a rich jus.
- **Scallops:** Delicately seared and served with a light, complementary sauce.
- **Vegetarian Risotto:** Creamy and packed with fresh, locally sourced vegetables.

Budget: Dining here falls into the mid-range category, with main courses generally costing between £15 and £30.

Additional Information: The ambience is cosy and rustic with modern touches. Reservations are recommended, particularly for dinner.

Kayal

Overview: Kayal is an authentic South Indian restaurant in Leamington Spa, a short drive from Warwick. Specializing in Keralan cuisine, Kayal offers a unique and flavourful dining experience with dishes that celebrate the rich culinary traditions of South India.

Best Dishes:

- **Masala Dosa:** A crispy rice pancake filled with spicy potato masala, served with coconut chutney and sambar.
- **Fish Curry:** Fresh fish cooked in a tangy and spicy coconut-based curry.
- **Vegetable Thali:** This dish consists of an assortment of vegetarian dishes served with rice and bread, perfect for sampling a variety of flavours.

Budget: Dining here is budget-friendly, with courses priced between £10 and £20.

Additional Information: The restaurant offers excellent options for vegetarians and vegans. Reservations are recommended, especially on weekends.

Other Warwick Eateries

Overview: Warwick has various excellent dining options, from casual cafés to fine dining restaurants. Here are a few noteworthy places:

- **Aqua Food & Mood:** An excellent Lebanese restaurant on Jury Street, known for its mezze platters, grilled meats, and vegetarian options. Main courses range from £10-£25.
- **Tailors Restaurant:** A fine dining spot on Market Place, offering a modern British menu with a creative twist. Try their tasting menu for a unique experience. Expect to spend around £50-£70 per person.
- **La Mesa:** A cosy Spanish tapas bar on Smith Street, perfect for sharing small plates of patatas bravas, chorizo, and seafood. Main tapas dishes cost around £5-£10 each.
- **The Art Kitchen:** Located on Swan Street, this Thai restaurant is renowned for its vibrant flavours and stylish presentation. Popular dishes include Pad Thai, green curry, and crispy duck. Mains range from £12-£20.

Exploring the best restaurants in Warwick and the surrounding areas will enhance your visit and offer a taste of the local culinary delights. Whether you're looking for a high-end dining experience or a casual meal, these recommendations provide something for everyone.

6

Best Hikes

W arwick and its surrounding areas offer a variety of beautiful hikes and walks that showcase the region's natural beauty and rich history. Within a 10-mile radius, there's something for everyone, whether you're looking for a leisurely stroll or a more challenging hike. Here are some of the best hikes, information on parking costs and other helpful tips.

Warwick Castle and River Avon Walk

Overview: This scenic walk takes you around the iconic Warwick Castle and the tranquil River Avon. It's perfect for those who want to combine history with natural beauty.
Route Details:

- Distance: 3 miles
- Difficulty: Easy
- Highlights: Views of Warwick Castle, the River Avon, and St. Nicholas Park.

Parking:

- St. Nicholas Park Car Park: £1 per hour.

Additional Information:

- Suitable for all ages and fitness levels.
- Great for picnics and photography.

Hatton Locks Walk

Overview: The Hatton Locks Walk is a delightful route along the Grand Union Canal, featuring a series of 21 locks known as the "Stairway to Heaven." It's a fascinating walk for those interested in engineering and nature.
Route Details:

- Distance: 4 miles
- Difficulty: Moderate

- Highlights: The flight of locks, canal boats, and scenic countryside views.

Parking:

- Hatton Locks Car Park: £2.50 for up to 4 hours, £5 for all day.

Additional Information:

- Suitable for moderate fitness levels.
- There's a café at the top of the locks for refreshments.

Kenilworth Castle and Abbey Fields

Overview: This walk combines historical exploration with natural beauty, taking you through the grounds of Kenilworth Castle and the surrounding Abbey Fields parkland.

Route Details:

- Distance: 2.5 miles
- Difficulty: Easy to moderate
- Highlights: Kenilworth Castle ruins, Abbey Fields, and the lake.

Parking:

- Kenilworth Castle Car Park: £2 for up to 2 hours, £4 for over 2 hours.

Additional Information:

- Suitable for families and history enthusiasts.

- Picnic areas are available in Abbey Fields.

Crackley Woods Nature Reserve

Overview: Crackley Woods offers a serene woodland walk with diverse wildlife and beautiful flora. It's a peaceful escape into nature, perfect for birdwatching and enjoying the outdoors.
Route Details:

- Distance: 2 miles
- Difficulty: Easy
- Highlights: Ancient woodland, wildflowers, and birdwatching opportunities.

Parking:

- Crackley Woods Car Park: Free parking is available at the entrance.

Additional Information:

- Suitable for all fitness levels.
- Wear sturdy shoes, as paths can be muddy.

The Mill Garden to Guys Cliffe Walk

Overview: This picturesque walk starts at the Mill Garden near Warwick Castle and follows the River Avon to the historic Guys Cliffe estate. It offers a mix of garden beauty and historical intrigue.
Route Details:

- Distance: 3.5 miles

- Difficulty: Moderate
- Highlights: Mill Garden, River Avon, and Guys Cliffe House ruins.

Parking:

- Mill Garden Parking: Street parking is available nearby; charges may vary.

Additional Information:

- Suitable for moderate fitness levels.
- Check the opening times for Mill Garden if you are planning to visit.

Welcombe Hills and Clopton Park

Overview: Located just outside Stratford-upon-Avon, this hike offers expansive views over the Warwickshire countryside, historical sites, and beautiful woodland areas.
  Route Details:

- Distance: 4 miles
- Difficulty: Moderate
- Highlights: Panoramic views, Welcombe Monument, and Clopton Tower.

Parking:

- Welcombe Hills Car Park: Free parking is available at the entrance.

Additional Information:

- Suitable for moderate fitness levels.
- Bring water and snacks, as there are limited facilities on the route.

Exploring these walks and hikes around Warwick will allow you to experience the region's natural beauty, historical landmarks, and charming countryside. Whether you're a seasoned hiker or just looking for a pleasant walk, these trails offer something for everyone.

7

Day Trips

W arwick is a charming destination and a fantastic base for exploring the surrounding areas. Within a 10-mile radius, there are numerous attractions and destinations worth visiting. This chapter highlights some of the best day trips, providing details on costs, budget considerations, and helpful tips.

Stratford-upon-Avon

Overview: Stratford-upon-Avon, the birthplace of William Shakespeare, is a must-visit for literature and history enthusiasts. This picturesque town offers a wealth of cultural and historical attractions.

Top Attractions:

- **Shakespeare's Birthplace:** Explore the house where Shakespeare was born and grew up. Admission: £18-£25.
- **Anne Hathaway's Cottage:** Visit the beautiful thatched cottage of Shakespeare's wife. Admission: £10-£15.
- **Royal Shakespeare Theatre:** Catch a play by the Royal Shakespeare Company. Tickets: £20-£60.

Budget Considerations:

- **Moderate to Expensive:** Depending on the activities you choose. Look for combo tickets to save on multiple attractions.
- **Dining:** A mix of budget-friendly cafés and high-end restaurants.

Additional Information:

- **Transportation:** Trains and buses run regularly from Warwick to Stratford-upon-Avon. Train fare: £5-£10 each way.

Kenilworth

Overview: Kenilworth is a historic town known for its impressive castle ruins and lovely parklands. It's perfect for a relaxed day trip filled with history and nature.

Top Attractions:

- **Kenilworth Castle**: Explore the extensive ruins and the beautiful Elizabethan Garden. Admission: £12-£15.
- **Abbey Fields:** A large park ideal for picnics, walks, and leisure activities. Free entry.

Budget Considerations:

- **Budget to Moderate:** Kenilworth Castle has an admission fee, but the rest of the town is free to explore.
- **Dining:** Options range from quaint tea rooms to family-friendly pubs.

Additional Information:

- **Transportation:** Easily accessible by bus from Warwick. Bus fare: £2-£5 each way.

Royal Leamington Spa

Overview: Royal Leamington Spa is renowned for its Regency architecture, beautiful parks, and vibrant shopping scene. It's a great spot for a leisurely day out.

Top Attractions:

- **Jephson Gardens:** Enjoy these beautifully landscaped gardens. Free entry.
- **Royal Pump Rooms:** Visit the museum and art gallery to learn about the town's spa history. Free entry.
- **Shopping:** Explore the eclectic mix of high-street shops, boutiques, and markets.

Budget Considerations:

- **Budget-Friendly:** Most attractions are free. Shopping and dining costs can vary.
- **Dining:** Plenty of affordable cafés, restaurants, and pubs.

Additional Information:
Transportation: A short bus or train ride from Warwick. Bus fare: £2-£4 each way.

Charlecote Park

Overview: Charlecote Park is a grand 16th-century country house surrounded by deer parks and gardens. Managed by the National Trust, it offers a glimpse into the past and beautiful natural scenery.
Top Attractions:

- **Charlecote House:** Tour the impressive house and its collections. Admission: £13-£15.
- **Deer Park:** Stroll through the park and enjoy watching the resident deer. Included with house admission.

Budget Considerations:

- **Moderate**: National Trust members get free entry; non-members pay an admission fee.
- **Dining**: The Café on-site offers refreshments and light meals.

Additional Information:

- **Transportation**: Best reached by car. Parking: £4 (free for National Trust members).

Compton Verney Art Gallery and Park

Overview: Compton Verney is an award-winning art gallery housed in a stunning Georgian mansion surrounded by landscaped parkland.
Top Attractions:

- **Art Gallery:** Exhibits range from historic to contemporary art. Admission: £10-£15.
- **Parkland:** Explore the 120 acres of beautiful grounds. Included with gallery admission.

Budget Considerations:

- **Moderate:** Admission fees apply, but discounts are available for families and students.
- **Dining:** The on-site café serves a variety of meals and snacks.

Additional Information:

- **Transportation:** Best reached by car. Parking: £3.

Hatton Country World

Overview: Hatton Country World offers a delightful day out for families. It combines a farm park with shopping and dining experiences.
Top Attractions:

- **Adventure World:** Farm animals, play areas, and seasonal activities. Admission: £12-£15.
- **Shopping Village:** Independent shops offering unique gifts and local produce. Free entry.

Budget Considerations:

- **Moderate:** Admission fees for the Adventure World; shopping and dining costs vary.
- **Dining:** Variety of cafés and food stalls.

Additional Information:

- **Transportation:** Accessible by car or bus. Parking is free.

Exploring these day trips from Warwick will enrich your visit with diverse experiences, from historic sites and cultural attractions to beautiful parks and family-friendly activities.

8

Best Family Activities

W arwick and its surrounding areas offer a wealth of family-friendly activities for all ages and interests. From historical attractions to outdoor adventures, there's something for everyone within a 10-mile radius. This chapter highlights the best family activities and details costs, budget considerations, and other helpful information.

Warwick Castle

Overview: Warwick Castle is a must-visit for families, offering an exciting blend of history, entertainment, and interactive experiences.
Top Activities:

- **Castle Tours:** Explore the grand interiors and learn about the castle's history.
- **The Princess Tower:** A magical experience for young children where they can help solve a riddle to save a princess.
- **Knight School:** Kids can learn the skills of a knight with fun, hands-on activities.
- **Falconry Displays:** Watch impressive birds of prey in action.

Budget Considerations:

- **Moderate to Expensive:** Admission ranges from £20 to £30 per person. Look for family tickets and online discounts.
- **Dining:** On-site eateries offer a range of options, but you can also bring a picnic.

Additional Information:

- **Duration:** Plan to spend at least half a day to enjoy all the activities fully.
- **Accessibility:** The castle is mostly accessible, but some areas may have limited access due to historical architecture.

St. Nicholas Park

Overview: St. Nicholas Park is a fantastic spot for a family day out. It offers a variety of activities in a beautiful setting.
Top Activities:

- **Playground:** A large, well-equipped play area for children.
- **Boating:** Rent pedal boats and enjoy the River Avon.
- **Mini Golf:** A fun and affordable mini-golf course.
- **Train Rides:** A small train that takes kids around the park.

Budget Considerations:

- **Budget-Friendly:** Entry to the park is free, but there are small fees for activities like boating and mini golf (around £3-£5 per person).

Additional Information:

- **Picnics:** Plenty of picnic spots are available.
- **Parking:** Pay-and-display parking is available on-site (£1 per hour).

Hatton Adventure World

Overview: Hatton Adventure World is an excellent choice for families with young children. It offers a mix of indoor and outdoor activities.
Top Activities:

- **Animal Farm:** Meet and feed various farm animals.
- **Indoor Play:** A large soft play area perfect for younger kids.
- **Outdoor Adventure:** Tractor rides, bouncy castles, and mazes.
- **Seasonal Events:** Special activities during holidays, like Easter egg

hunts and Christmas festivities.

Budget Considerations:

- **Moderate:** Admission is around £12-£15 per person; family tickets are available.
- **Dining:** On-site cafés provide meals and snacks, or bring your picnic.

Additional Information:

- **Duration:** Plan for a full day to enjoy all the activities.
- **Accessibility:** Generally accessible, with facilities for young children and families.

Jephson Gardens

Overview: Located near Leamington Spa, Jephson Gardens is a beautiful park with plenty of family-friendly features.
Top Activities:

- **Play Area:** A well-maintained playground for kids.
- **Glasshouse:** Explore exotic plants and small wildlife.
- **Paddle Boats:** Rent boats on the lake.
- **Gardens and Trails:** Enjoy walking through the beautifully landscaped gardens.

Budget Considerations:

- **Budget-Friendly:** Entry to the park is free; small fees for activities like paddle boats (around £3-£5).

Additional Information:

- **Picnics:** Ample space for picnics and outdoor games.
- **Parking:** Pay-and-display parking nearby (£1-£2 per hour).

Stratford Butterfly Farm

Overview: Stratford Butterfly Farm is a magical place a short drive from Warwick. Here, families can experience tropical butterflies up close.

Top Activities:

- **Butterfly House:** Walk among free-flying butterflies in a tropical environment.
- **Minibeast Metropolis:** Learn about spiders, insects, and other creepy crawlies.
- **Discovery Zone:** Educational exhibits about the lifecycle and habitats of butterflies.

Budget Considerations:

- **Moderate:** Admission is around £7-£9 per person; family tickets available.
- **Dining:** Small café on-site, or bring a picnic to enjoy outside.

Additional Information:

- **Duration:** Plan for a few hours to half a day.
- **Accessibility:** Fully accessible for pushchairs and wheelchairs.

Ryton Pools Country Park

Overview: Ryton Pools Country Park offers a fantastic outdoor experience with activities for all ages.

Top Activities:

- **Nature Trails:** Various walking and cycling trails through woodland and around lakes.
- **Play Area:** Large play area for children.
- **Wildlife Watching:** Plenty of opportunities to spot local wildlife.
- **Visitor Centre:** Interactive exhibits and information about the park.

Budget Considerations:

- **Budget-Friendly:** Entry to the park is free; parking costs £3 daily.

Additional Information:

Picnics: Designated picnic areas with tables.

- **Facilities:** Toilets and baby changing facilities are available.

Exploring these family-friendly activities around Warwick ensures something enjoyable for everyone. From historical adventures to outdoor fun, your family will create lasting memories during your visit.

9

Conclusion

From exploring the historic grandeur of Warwick Castle and strolling through the charming town centre to savouring delicious local cuisine and enjoying family-friendly activities, Warwick offers many experiences that cater to every interest and age. The surrounding areas, with their scenic hikes, delightful day trips, and vibrant dining scene, further enrich your travel experience.

Whether immersing yourself in the rich history of Stratford-upon-Avon, wandering the serene paths of Jephson Gardens, or indulging in the culinary delights of Warwick's top restaurants, each moment spent here will surely create lasting memories.

As you navigate your adventures, remember the practical tips shared throughout this guide, from packing appropriately for the UK's variable weather to efficiently getting around town and beyond. Remember, prices can vary depending on individual choices. Adjustments can be made according to personal preferences, but this book gives a baseline for what you might expect to spend on a memorable trip to Warwick. Always search for combined deals to get the best prices. With thoughtful planning and a spirit of exploration, you're set for an unforgettable journey.

Warwick is a destination that seamlessly blends historic charm with modern comforts, offering a unique and memorable experience. We hope this guide has inspired you to explore every corner of this beautiful region and enjoy all it offers. Safe travels and happy exploring!

10

Resources

Top restaurant reviews | The Good Food Guide. (n.d.). Retrieved May 15, 2024, from https://www.thegoodfoodg uide.co.uk/search.

Tripadvisor. (n.d.). *Restaurants in Warwick - Trip Advisor*. Retrieved May 15, 2024, from https://www.tripadvisor.co.uk/FindRestaurants?geo=1 86400&sort=RELEVANCE&broadened=false

OpenAI. (2024). ChatGPT (Version GPT-4) [Large language model]. Retrieved May 23, 2024, from https://chat.openai.com

Printed in Dunstable, United Kingdom

66504329R10040